SMALL SPACES

SMALL SPACES

Edited by Cristina Paredes Benítez

COLLINS|DESIGN

An Imprint of HarperCollins*Publishers*

First Edition
Published by Loft Publications in 2005
Via Laietana, 32
08003 Barcelona. Spain
www.loftpublications.com

English language edition first published in 2005 by:
Collins Design,
An Imprint of HarperCollins*Publishers*
10 East 53rd Street
New York, NY 10022
Tel.: (212) 207-7000
Fax: (212) 207-7654
collinsdesign@harpercollins.com
www.harpercollins.com

Distributed throughout the world by:
HarperCollins*Publishers*
10 East 53rd Street
New York, NY 10022
Fax: (212) 207-7654

Executive editor:
Paco Asensio

Editorial coordination & Texts:
Cristina Paredes Benítez

Translation:
Matthew Clarke

Art director:
Mireia Casanovas Soley

Graphic design and layout:
Cris Tarradas Dulcet

Cover photo: Jordi Miralles
Backcover photo: Shania Shegedyn

Library of Congress Cataloging-in-Publication Data

Paredes, Cristina.
  Small Spaces: Good Ideas / by Cristina Paredes.
    p. cm.
  ISBN 0-06-083337-8 (pbk.)
  1. Lofts. 2. Interior decoration. 3. Interior architecture. I. Title.
  NK2117.L63B34 2005
  747.7'9--dc22
                        2005007821

Printed in Barcelona, Spain
Anman Gràfiques del Vallès
DL: B-35.971-2005

First printing, 2005

Contents

Introduction

The modern lifestyle and the changes that have occurred in society since the nineteenth century have led people to live in increasingly small spaces. The population boom in cities, combined with their inability to expand further in many cases, has resulted in a shortage of floor space, resulting in an increase in housing prices. This situation obliges people living alone—such as young people in their first home—to opt for a small house or apartment, or a loft.

There are many practical resources available when it comes to living comfortably in a small space: for example, in new buildings or conversions, it is possible to eliminate rooms that are not essential, such as hallways and corridors, and add the saved space to the main living area. Custom-designed furniture is another good option, as it always conforms to the taste of the occupants. Similarly, a single space is often assigned various uses, enabling a sitting room, for example, to also serve as a studio and bedroom. A design that takes advantage of simple lines, interplays of light or a color scheme all offer different ways of changing the appearance of rooms: thus, pale colors heighten the sensation of expansiveness and luminosity, while a few splashes of bright color can imbue a space with personality. Furthermore, some architectural and decorative styles, such as minimalism, are inherently favorable to the creation of simple, open spaces.

This book offers a collection of original, imaginative projects with a maximum area of 970 square feet. They include various types of homes: modules, refurbished apartments, or small, newly built houses. In short, a thousand and one ideas for taking the maximum advantage of the space available and enjoying a high quality of life.

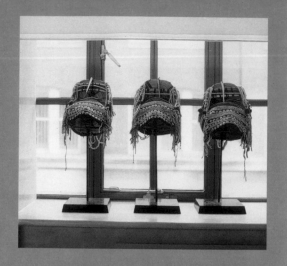

Studio in Covent Garden

150 sq.ft.

This small studio is located in an area once dominated by warehouses in Covent Garden, the London neighborhood that contains the Royal Opera House. The refurbishment sought to convert an anonymous space into the owner's office while also enabling it to serve domestic purposes. The first step consisted in changing the color scheme, using neutral colors to convey softness and serenity. The windows allow light to penetrate into the interior— something of a luxury for a London residence. The functional furniture, integrated into the lounge, makes it possible to close off the office area and hide a bed, while also creating a comfortable, welcoming atmosphere. The decoration, characterized by the simplicity of its elements, clearly attests to the owner's Asian origins.

Interior Designer: René Dekker

Location: London, UK

Completion date: 2003

Photographer: © James Silverman

The bedroom consists of a folding bed that occupies the space used as a dining room by day. The unit hiding the bed contains several closets and is spread across the entire wall. All the furniture has been designed to maximize the space and avoid the need to move any elements if the office area or bed is required for use. The application of soft colors helps to create a relaxing atmosphere that exudes harmony.

Optibo

270 sq.ft.

The lack of space and urban expansion augurs a future in which most houses will be on a small scale. Optibo is an original concept that makes it possible to enjoy an uncramped home in only 270 square feet. The secret lies in adapting the space to the use required at any particular time. Some pieces of furniture can be lowered and hidden in the floor, using an electric hydraulic system: the dining table and bed can appear or disappear as needed. One of the main assets of Optibo is its use of technology and materials that respect the environment, such as fiber optics and LED for the lighting. This prototype was designed in accordance with the Agenda 21 program, adopted by the UN at its conference in Rio de Janeiro in 1992.

Architects: White Architects, White Design

Location: mobile

Completion date: 2003

Photographers: © Bert Leandersonn, Richard Lindor

The electric hydraulic system makes it possible to effortlessly raise or lower the bed and table; the technological resources available also make it possible to graduate the height of the furniture or the intensity of the light. This adaptation of the space makes it possible to achieve comfort and expansiveness.

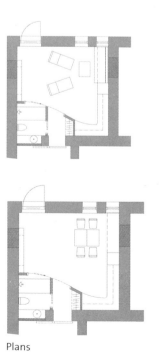

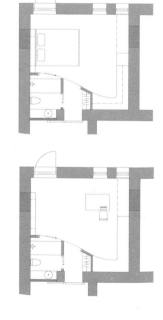

The bathroom also has surprises: the shower is set in one corner, but the wooden planks on the floor can be removed to reveal a bathtub underneath. This element was included to take advantage of the fact that the house is raised, which makes it possible to benefit from a more complete bathroom.

Plans

Houseboat

323 sq.ft.

Living in a floating house offers many advantages: panoramic views and the chance to take a dip or move to a quieter spot at any time—all possible in this small home moored off the west coast of Sweden. The architect's main aim was to create spacious rooms flooded with light. A wall with sliding doors and a glass roof open the living area on to the exterior, even on rainy days. This aquatic home boasts a living room, bedrooms, a bathroom, office and kitchen—which also serves as an access area to the rest of the home—as well as modern conveniences: extensive equipment in the kitchen, a log stove, and even a sauna. The flexible layout and the simple, versatile furniture are the keys to the success of this small space.

Architect: Rolf Åsberg

Location: Gothenburg, Sweden

Completion date: 2001

Photographer: © James Silverman

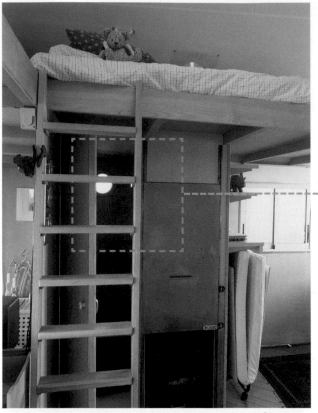

One of the most common strategies in small homes is to avoid leaving any space unused. Accordingly, the space below one of the bedrooms has been used to house the sauna and log stove; the latter warms the whole boat and provides the heat required by the sauna. The functional space separating the living room from the office is also exploited with similar ingenuity.

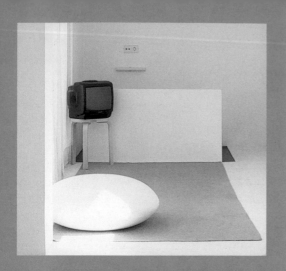

Apartment in Janelas Verdes

323 sq.ft.

This small apartment in central Lisbon is split into two levels. It presented one immediate and significant problem: a lack of light. As there are no façades that gave on to the exterior (apart from a small entrance in a small inner patio), sunlight scarcely penetrated inside, emphasizing the already limited dimensions. In order to gain a sense of spaciousness, the first step was to paint the walls, ceilings, and floors white. Large windows were fitted to increase the influx of light and focus attention on the tree in the patio. The lounge also serves as a transit area, and as a result the furnishings are minimal. The bedroom is set on the lower level of the apartment, with access to the patio, via a small, dark-colored staircase that contrasts with the paleness of the rest of the apartment.

Architect: João Maria Ventura

Collaborator: Nuno Pinto

Location: Lisbon, Portugal

Completion date: 2001

Photographer: © Sergio Mah

The lounge has been set in a transit area, thereby reclaiming a space that normally lacks any specific use. As it is situated in front of the window looking onto the patio, it also receives abundant light; it is undoubtedly one of the refurbished areas in which the sense of expansiveness is most apparent.

Sections

Lower level

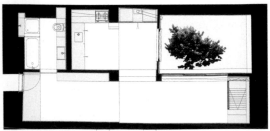

Upper level

All in a Cabinet

323 sq.ft.

The essential characteristics of this small apartment were its regular proportions and high ceiling. The architects took advantage of these two features to put against one wall a large sycamore-wood unit containing a bed, closet, and worktable, as well as space for the fax machine, music system, and television. The wooden panels do not reach the ceiling, allowing natural light to penetrate into the bedroom and thereby emphasizing the continuity and spaciousness. Bright colors were chosen to add vitality and counteract the underlying sobriety of the apartment. The lounge is set at one end, dominated by an old fireplace that the architects decided to retain, as it establishes a contrast with the modernity of the rest of the space and adds a touch of character.

Architect: Guillaume Server & Fabienne Couvert

Location: Paris, France

Completion date: 2000

Photographer: © Vicent Lerroux/ACI Roca Sastre

One way of taking advantage of small spaces is to fit bookcases into irregular areas. In this case, they have been placed on both sides of the fireplace to store not only books but also compact discs. These bookcases fit perfectly into the contours of the building and avoid overburdening the space with an excess of furniture.

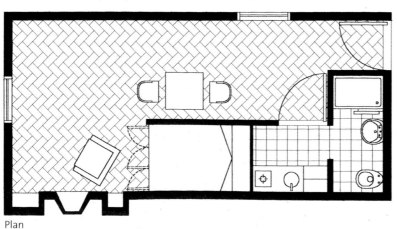

Plan

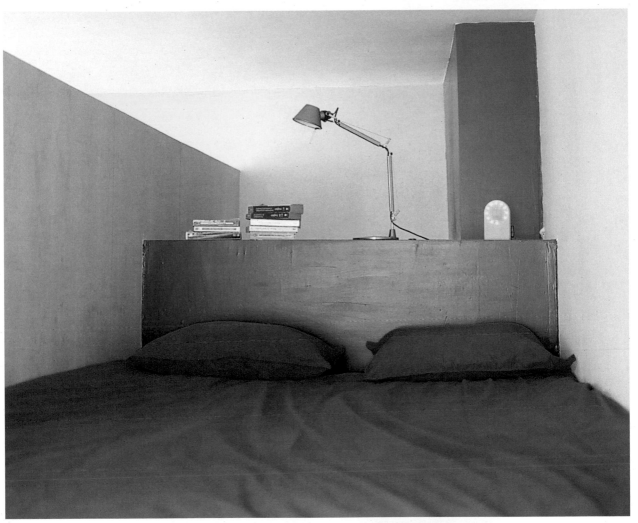

All in One Unit

320 sq.ft.

The refurbishment of this small apartment measuring a mere 320 square feet posed a considerable challenge. Despite its limited size, the main objective—to achieve a functional apartment with a leisure area—was fulfilled by reducing the dimensions of the kitchen and bathroom areas to the minimum and making the lounge, studio, bedroom, and projection room share the same space. The separation between the two areas was modified, leaving only a half-height partition that allows sunlight to pour in. The predominance of white provides further luminosity and helps create a sense of spaciousness. Similarly, the white drapes and fluorescent lamps set up an interplay of lights and transparencies that modifies the atmosphere of the home.

Architect: Gary Chang/EDGE

Location: Hong Kong, China

Completion date: 2000

Photographer: © Almond Chu

The one and only window, on the rear façade, allows light to penetrate into the apartment, especially into the studio area and bedroom. In small spaces, particular emphasis should be placed on the areas with the greatest amount of activity, so the dimensions of the kitchen and bathroom were reduced to a minimum. The bookcases and closets are hidden behind white drapes that can display or hide the interior as required.

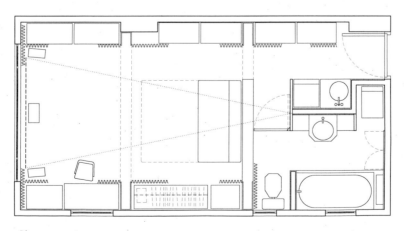

Plan

The refurbishment project required the installation of projection facilities. The large extending screen has been placed in front of the window to take advantage of the only free wall; it can also be used as a television or computer screen. The drapes that hide the closets and the diffuse light at floor level add a theatrical touch to the setting.

Layer House

355 sq.ft.

The main aim of this project was to build a house as comfortable and spacious as possible on a very small lot. The architect, who is also the owner of the house, created a structure based on alternating concrete strips, which is both extremely solid and easy on the eye. The strips, arranged in the form of a trellis, allow light to enter. The wood used inside the house combines with the tree in the entrance to conjure up an organic, natural feel that is warmer and less aggressive than many Japanese buildings. The various parts of the home were separated according to the required degree of intimacy, and it is surprising how much space was attained by establishing a number of different levels, joined together by steps inserted into the empty spaces between the strips.

Architect: Hiroaki Ohtani
Location: Kobe, Japan
Completion date: 2003
Photographer: © Kouji Okamoto

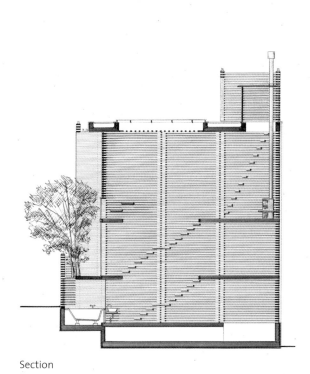

Section

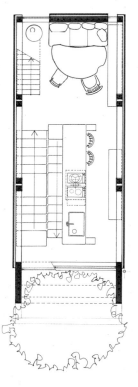

Floor plan

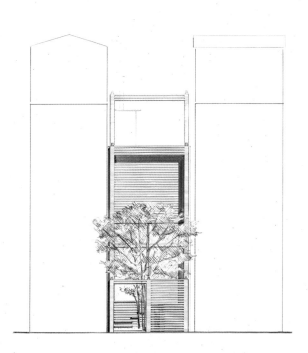

Elevation

The rooms are spread over different levels and connected by steps that occupy the least possible space and are made even more unobtrusive by being fixed to the wall. Wood has been used to create a warm, cozy atmosphere, complemented by the light that filters into the house through the gaps between the strips on the roof. ━━━━━━━

Monolocal

387 sq.ft.

The floor space here spans a mere 194 square feet, while the height ranges from 36 to 58 feet, making it possible to create two distinct levels. The bathroom is the only space that is closed off; the rest of the house is completely open in order to endow the space with continuity. The first level is occupied by the bathroom, kitchen-dining room, and lounge; the bedroom and closets are set on the upper level, reached by a steep staircase. The ensemble is painted in several intensities of white, and the variety of shades increases the feeling of spaciousness. The play of light, both natural and artificial, also emphasizes this sensation and contributes to the minimalism of this home.

Architect: Studio Associato Bettinelli

Location: Milan, Italy

Completion date: 2003

Photographer: © Andrea Martiradonna

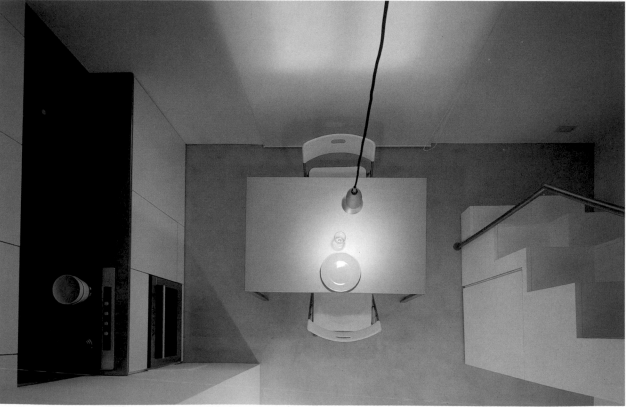

The lighting in this home is simple but effective. The two skylights allow light to flood into the bedroom and kitchen area, while both the top level and the lounge area have been adorned with small square lamps.

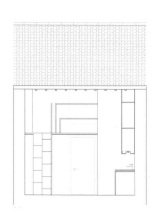

Section

Sections

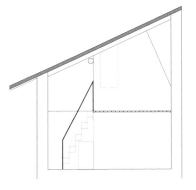

Plan

Hanse Colani Rotorhaus

387 sq.ft.

The aim of this prefabricated house was to achieve the maximum possible amount of interior space in a confined floor area. In order to cover all the needs of a modern house, an ingenious solution was formulated: one single space would perform various functions. The kitchen, bedroom, and part of the bathroom are set in a rotating cylinder with an innovative, futuristic design; it rotates to expose the area required at any particular time. The living room containing the cylinder complements all the other spaces in the home, making them seem much bigger. Rotorhaus and the architect Luigi Colani designed this house with a young, mobile public in mind; they have managed to combine functionality with design, demonstrating that prefabricated houses and creativity are not mutually exclusive.

Architect: Luigi Colani, Hanse Haus

Location: Oberleichtersbach, Germany

Completion date: 2004

Photographer: © Hanse Haus GmbH

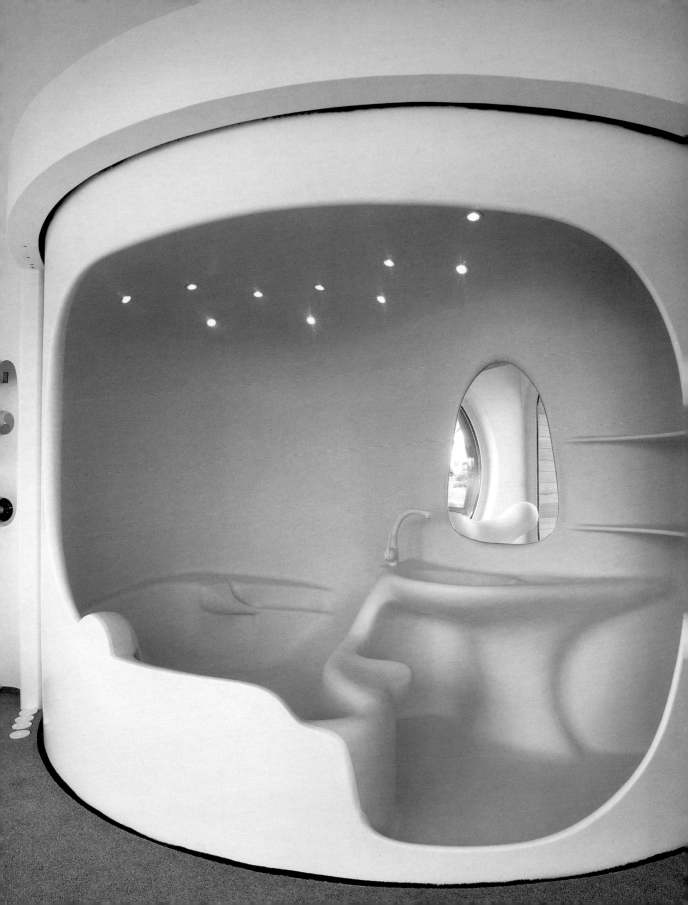

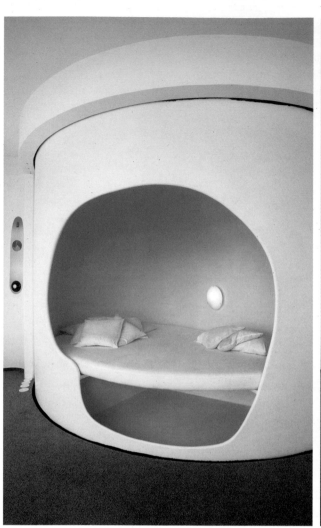

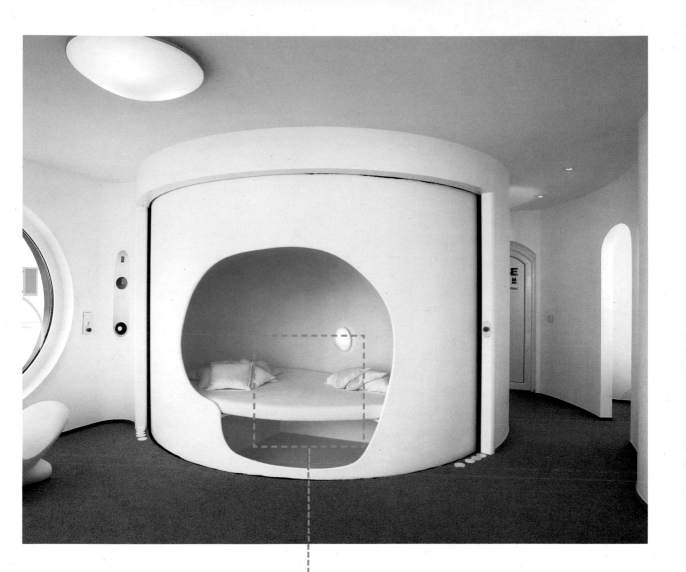

Each of the areas in the cylinder has a different color, to accentuate the youthful, futuristic atmosphere of the interior. The bed in the pale pink bedroom sleeps two people. The synthetic materials contrast with the wood of the exterior structure, which gives the house a welcoming, rustic look.

Loftcube

420 sq.ft.

The creators of the Loftcube define it as a temporary, minimalist home. This module is specially aimed at young people accustomed to an urban lifestyle and free to move from place to place as circumstances require. The Loftcube is intended as a solution to the problem of finding affordable accommodation in large cities, so it is designed to be set up on roofs to take advantage of a space that is normally left empty. It can even be transported by helicopter. It can be assembled easily and quickly; the interior can be organized according to the tastes of the owner or tenant, who chooses the color, quality of the materials, and even the placement of the mobile panels. The colorful, youthful furniture helps to create a warm, personal, and modern setting.

Architect: Werner Aisslinger/Studio Aisslinger

Location: mobile

Completion date: 2004

Photographer: © Steffen Jänicke & Jens Vogt

The interior of this loft is subdivided with panels made of synthetic materials from DuPont that slide on rails and organize the layout of the living space. The furniture, consisting of portable modules, is adjusted to the interior spaces and serves various functions: the shower, for example, is also a watering system for plants.

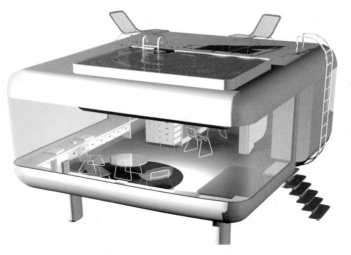

Rendering

Smart Apartment

430 sq.ft.

The refurbishment of this small studio in a 1920s building in the center of Sydney has turned an uncomfortable studio into a one-bedroom apartment. An "artistic" wall, the work of Tim Richardson, was installed to separate the living room from the bedroom, allowing the latter to become an extension of the living room and emphasizing the flexibility of this minimalist home. A lacquered red unit serves as a container for all the electrical appliances and closets while maintaining the unity of the apartment. The original tiles in the bathroom have been retained, along with the window frames, to achieve a greater visual impact. Despite its limited dimensions, the apartment appears spacious and bright, thanks to the sunshine and the use of simple lines in the design.

Architect: Smart Design Studio

Location: Sydney, Australia

Completion date: 2002

Photographer: © Sharrin Rees

The electrical appliances and closets are paneled to avoid disrupting the uniformity of the setting. In this case, the closets act as a compact blade, revealing or hiding the tools. Made of lacquered red wood, it is far more than a mere series of closets, for it constitutes an original piece with a personality all its own.

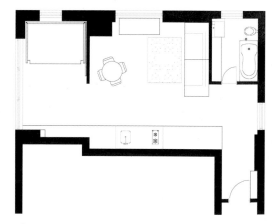

Plan

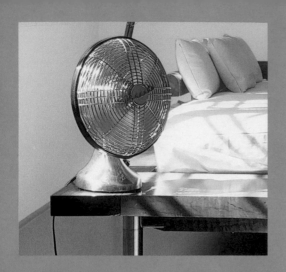

Miami White

484 sq.ft.

The refurbishment of this small studio belonging to an architect has turned it into a single space with a distinctive, youthful style. White predominates throughout, broken only by a few well-calculated splashes of color that create an original and cheerful atmosphere. The bedroom doubles as a living room, with the bed serving as a highly versatile piece of furniture. The wooden support on which the mattress is set juts out slightly; it is used to store books and other objects, including an arched lamp. These elements round off the organization of the room and accentuate its multifunctionality. The small but practical kitchen is situated behind one of the few walls in the studio, while the small office contains a desk, a compact unit on rollers for storing papers, and a methacrylate chair that goes almost unnoticed.

Architect: Studio Uribe

Location: Miami, FL, USA

Completion date: 2000

Photographer: © Pep Escoda

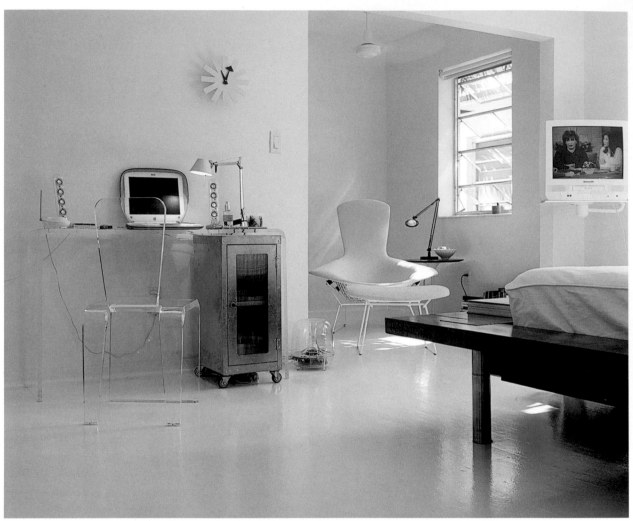

The kitchen is set behind one of the studio's partitions and is practically invisible from the bed. In this predominantly white area, a small refrigerator with a glass door also serves as a work top. A reading corner has been set up in front of the kitchen, with a comfortable armchair that personalizes the decoration of the studio still further.

Careful planning and a touch of ingenuity are required to structure and decorate small spaces; in such cases, a particular area or piece of furniture can serve several functions. The bed is a good example of this; the addition of armrests and cushions turns it into a couch for guests or a lounge space for reading or listening to music.

Apartment in Shepherd's Bush

506 sq.ft.

The refurbishment of this small apartment in London had two main objectives: the incorporation of a working space and the means to fit all the necessary electrical appliances in the kitchen. A worktable, hidden behind a large closet in the bedroom, is capable of holding a large amount of clothes, shoes, and other objects. This closet was deliberately not allowed to reach either the floor or the ceiling, making it seem lighter and maintaining the austerity of the overall design. The walls are painted white to reflect light and give a sense of spaciousness, although a few touches of lilac on the kitchen work top and the decorative elements add warmth and offset the coldness inherent in white when it is used as the predominant color.

Architect: Jeremy King

Location: London, UK

Completion date: 2000

Photographer: © Montse Garriga

The wooden shelves on both sides of the old fireplace provide space for storing books and compact discs. All the pieces of furniture placed in the apartment were carefully chosen to avoid cluttering up the space.

Subtle details set off a decorative scheme that would otherwise be extremely minimalist; the touches of lilac and use of wood and natural fabrics create a simple but welcoming setting. The kitchen counter, which also serves as bar for eating, runs into the sitting room, where it turns into a bookshelf.

This closet attached to the wall is undoubtedly one of the most effective additions to the apartment: during the day, two tip-up doors can be used as a worktable, while at night the closet can be closed and the bedroom recovers its normal appearance. The closet does not occupy the whole wall, only the central part, to prevent it from being too prominent.

Itamar Cave

538 sq.ft.

This cave in Jerusalem has been converted into a small home, adjusted to the space available. The stone walls have barely been altered, to preserve a rustic look and spark off a dialogue with the exterior. The refurbishment, designed and undertaken by the owners, sought to preserve the essential features of the cave: the walls are irregular and the colors used, both inside and outside, are natural and earthy. No divisions have been set between the rooms, in order to open up the home and also maintain the feel of the original cave. The furniture constitutes the minimum required to live in comfort; all superfluous decoration has been avoided, as this would detract from the naturalness of this little house.

Designers: Owners

Location: Jerusalem, Israel

Completion date: 2004

Photographer: © Yael Pincus

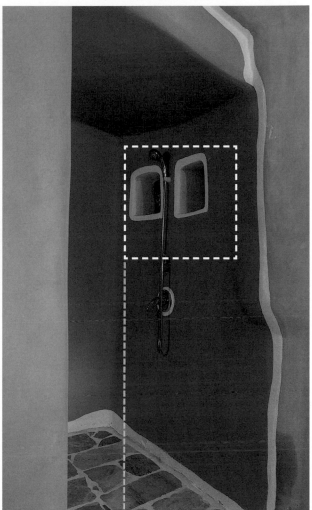

The bathroom area is painted bright blue, which contrasts with the earth color of the living room and kitchen. The various areas of the house are differentiated by means of colors, obviating any need for separations. As a result, nothing is allowed to disrupt the continuity of the space.

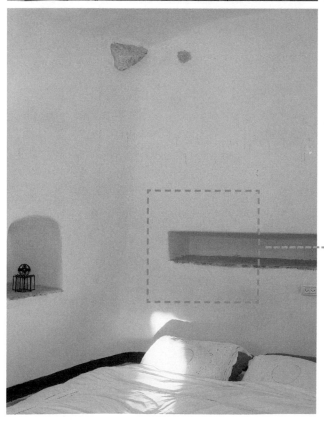

The only bedroom in the house is very austerely decorated. The mattress lies on the floor and the furniture is limited to one small standard lamp. White has been used to create an atmosphere full of calm and purity, while the niches in the wall provide a rustic touch with a decorative effect.

Seefels Apartment

538 sq.ft.

The aim of the enlargement of this apartment next to Lake Worther was to achieve the maximum comfort possible in such a limited space. One of the main changes occurred in the kitchen, which has incorporated all its essential features into a small unit fitted into the wall. The decoration is very austere, while the contrast between the color of the teakwood and the white of the sofas and drapes endows the apartment with a modern, minimalist look. The only purely decorative element is the original lighting setup in the living area. The apartment is divided into two areas: while the bedroom was conceived as an intimate, private space, the living room has been converted into an open area with various uses and functions.

Architect: BEHF Architekten

Location: Kränten, Austria

Completion date: 2003

Photographer: © Rupert Steiner

This project takes advantage of a long wall to fit in the closets and kitchen area, with the same teakwood used elsewhere in the house. The passageway has been narrowed in the process, with only a small part remaining visible (framed in white to provide more luminosity, as well as to add a decorative touch).

The couches and upholstered walls in the living room are fitted with a lighting system that can change the atmosphere and adapt it to different requirements. White is the dominant color, as it is present on both the walls and the drapes, thereby brightening up the space.

As in the bedroom, white predominates in the bathroom, making them the most luminous areas of the home. Particularly worthy of note are the robust white washbasins and the frosted-glass partition, which marks off the shower area (reached via a swing door).

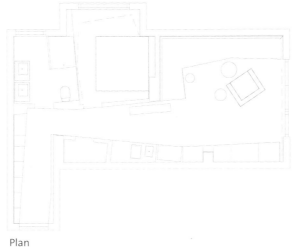

Plan

Flat in Castiglione

538 sq.ft.

This home in the historic center of Castiglione delle Stiviere has been designed for a young couple that shares an intense interest in design and a passion for dance and choreography. At first sight, it seems to be an open, modern space, with no conventional partitions, but, in reality, the classic areas in a home—the bedroom, bathroom, and kitchen, for example—are clearly marked out by means of compact cubes, thereby setting up a dialogue between the modernity of the home and the tenets of a traditional lifestyle. The cube that marks off the bedroom and the light bookcase, both mobile, were created by the architects; they are intended to make the space more adaptable and leave room for dancing and putting on small-scale performances.

Architect: Studio Rodighiero Associati

Location: Castiglione delle Stiviere, Italy

Completion date: 2004

Photographer: © Antonio de Luca & Alessandro Lui

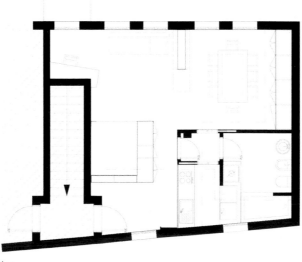

Plan

In small homes, ingenuity is required to take maximum advantage of the space. A clear example of this is the bedroom, where a cube-shape piece of furniture hides some drawers in its bottom section, making it possible to store a wide range of objects. The custom-made furniture is designed to the owners' specific requirements.

A small opening links the hall with the kitchen, allowing light to pass from one space to the other and energizing both of them. The distinctive silhouettes of trees painted on the walls bestow personality on the hall and establish continuity between the passageway and the lounge.

Mill House

538 sq.ft.

The Mill House is a small home inspired by both Oriental and Scandinavian traditions. The house is integrated into nature by means of its simple lines. Inside, there are no walls to disrupt the continuity of the space; materials such as wood and limestone define the different zones, but the expansive main area is left open. The kitchen is small but well designed and prominently placed in the living area; the couches around the fireplace create a cozy feel. The bedroom, with its double-slope ceiling, occupies the entire upper floor and creates a very warm atmosphere. The house has many conveniences, including a sauna, and the sensation of comfort is enhanced by the impressive natural surroundings, which can be seen from inside through the large window stretching across one wall.

Architect: Wingårdh Arkitektkontor

Location: Skåne, Sweden

Completion date: 2000

Photographer: © James Silverman

The absence of high closets in the kitchen creates an open space that bestows fluidity on the interior, as well as providing the opportunity to survey the rest of the home: the fireplace and the couches, the corridor leading to the bathroom and sauna, the exit onto the garden, and so on. The kitchen is not only a work space but also a transit area that links all the interior spaces.

The simplicity of the building's lines helps to set off the materials and high-quality finishing. The combination of limestone and wood—a cold and warm material, respectively—create an inviting atmosphere marked by tradition. Apart from these two materials, glass is used in the doors to allow sunlight to penetrate and to open the house to the exterior.

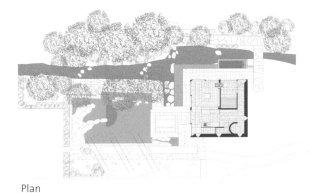

Plan

The bedroom on the top floor seems like a small refuge, warm and welcoming. Wood is the dominant material, but a large window allows in sunlight to create a tranquil, harmonious setting. The double-slope roof is remarkable for its pure, simple lines, typical of the entire house.

Summer House in Grunsen

538 sq.ft.

This small summer house, situated in a quiet area on the west coast of Sweden, forms part of a residential complex. The owners wanted a simple type of construction, but one made with high-quality materials, so that the house could "grow old gracefully." The brief also demanded the preservation of the essential characteristics of the site (an old farm). With these two premises in mind, the architects created a home with a flowing layout unimpeded by interruptions. Another important factor is the presence or absence of light, as the glass wall opens the house to its surroundings, while the exterior doors are opaque, to provide privacy and protection from the summer heat. Wood is used to particularly striking effect to supply warmth and coziness throughout the interior.

Architect: Peter Hulting/Meter Arkitektur

Location: Grunsen, Sweden

Completion date: 2004

Photographer: © James Silverman

This house is virtually a single space, with only the bathrooms enclosed and the bedroom bounded by a closet to afford greater privacy. The areas with the most social activity are all open, making it possible, for example, for the owners to chat with their guests while they are cooking in the kitchen zone. The furniture is reduced to essentials to ensure the continuity of the space.

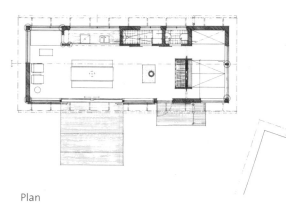

Plan

Apartment in Rome

500 sq.ft.

The refurbishment of this apartment mainly sought to take full advantage of both the floor area and the natural light. The previous layout was conventional and lacked character. The central area was overhauled to create an oval platform that takes in the kitchen and the bathroom. In this way, the open kitchen is integrated into the sitting room, while circulation areas have been created to provide a sense of expansiveness. This effect is enhanced by the use of white and the insertion of glass-brick walls, which allow light to enter the bathroom and kitchen. The furniture is sparse and simple, but the contrast between the colors of the carpets and the cushions imbue the setting with personality. The bold design softens the lines and emphasizes the originality of this home.

Architect: Massimo d'Alessandro & Associati

Location: Rome, Italy

Completion date: 2002

Photographer: © Andrea Martiradonna

The large windows of the apartment allow abundant light to pour into one area. The glass-brick walls, however, serve to distribute it throughout the rest of the house, while also preserving privacy. Similarly, the transit area also enables light to penetrate into the hall; furthermore, the oval walls do not reach the ceiling, bestowing a sense of continuity on the entire home.

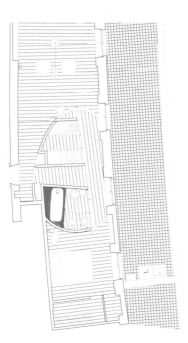

Plan

Apartment in Chelsea

570 sq.ft.

The refurbishment of this one-bedroom apartment involved the creation of a work area, a change in the layout of the kitchen, and the modification of some partitions. The walls have been replaced by mobile panels to provide fluidity, as well as to gain luminosity and views of the exterior. These panels make it possible to rearrange the layout at will and benefit from an open, comfortable space, according to the needs of the moment. The small office has been put in the area once occupied by a closet, and some pieces of furniture in the living room and bedroom have been made to measure—efficient and functional solutions that take maximum advantage of the space.

Architect: Rafael Berkowitz/RB Architect

Location: New York, USA

Completion date: 2003

Photographer: © James Wilkins

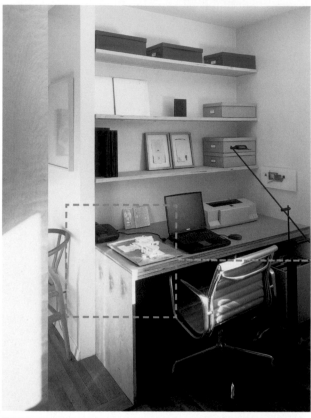

A closet has been replaced by the office, and three shelves have been added to it, running across the length of the wall. The office forms part of the bedroom, but it can be linked to the daytime area because partitions were removed during the refurbishment. The mobile panels can also be closed to achieve greater intimacy.

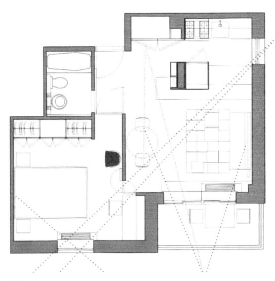

Plan

Modulable Apartment

570 sq.ft.

The refurbishment of this Parisian apartment, built in 1968, sought to adapt the space to the current needs of the owners while preserving the rationalism of the original construction. The three main aims were to increase the amount of storage space, take fuller advantage of natural light, and change the layout (as this was extremely unbalanced). To endow the whole apartment with more sunshine, the original diagonal partitions were removed and the walls were painted white to reflect the light. The mobile wood panels can be combined to give a sense of continuity between the different spaces, all of limited dimensions. A feeling of expansiveness is also achieved by the minimal furniture and the distribution of the closets, almost all fitted into the wall.

Architect: Guilhem Roustan

Location: Paris, France

Completion date: 2002

Photographer: © Alejandro Bahamón

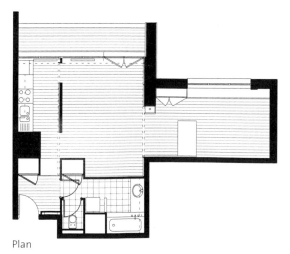

Plan

Sliding panels are a good option for small spaces; here, for example, a wooden panel makes it possible to close off the studio and bedroom and thereby create greater intimacy. The panels serve to separate the daytime area, such as the sitting room and kitchen, and the private or nighttime areas, such as the studio and the bedroom; they can also be withdrawn completely, however, to reveal the space in its entirety.

Dwelling in New York

570 sq.ft.

The main aim of the refurbishment of this small apartment was to install a graphic designer's office and home in an area measuring a mere 570 square feet. In order to do this, a distinctive wooden unit was inserted to separate the bedroom from the living room. This appears to be a solid box, but when the wooden panels are withdrawn, two complete desks are revealed and the couch that doubles as a bed for guests is hidden from view. The panels also have an opening that is lined up with the window in the living room, allowing natural light to penetrate into the office. Similarly, the dining-room table can slide toward the wall to make more space available for the office.

Architect: Roger Hirsch

Location: New York, USA

Completion date: 2002

Photographer: © Minh & Wass Photography

In working hours, the panels are slid back to reveal the desks inside the box, while for the rest of the day this space is occupied by a sofa bed; this unit, designed by the architects, is undoubtedly an original and practical solution to the problem of limited space.

Plan

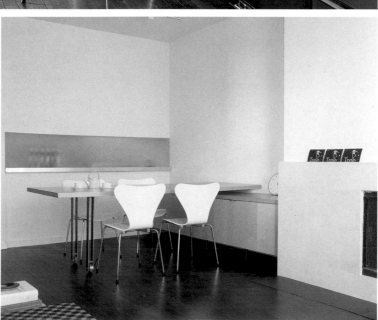

Fagelstraat

592 sq.ft.

The i29 team works in both architecture and furniture design, specializing in creating large spaces that assemble the basic services of a home into a single compact unit made to measure. This small apartment has been totally refurbished to endow it with greater modernity and space; it is long and thin, with a central module separating the entrance from the living area. It proved possible to combine the kitchen, bathroom, and closets into one solid but elegant unit with pure, simple lines. The furniture design has also been personalized to satisfy all the client's specific requirements, always respecting their relative degree of importance. The Fagelstraat project undoubtedly serves to illustrate one of the mottos of i29: less is more.

Architect: i29 Office for Spatial Design

Location: Amsterdam, Netherlands

Completion date: 2003

Photographer: © Jeroen Dellensen

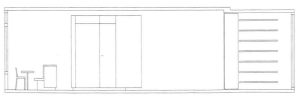

Section

Plan

The use of polyester and resins made it possible to create elements made from one single piece, such as the washbasin. They have been spray-painted to achieve a cleaner finish. The closets were not fitted with handles, to emphasize their autonomy.

Interlocking Puzzle

603 sq.ft.

The architects of this small loft in New York have managed to fit together various volumes to achieve a tight-fitting jigsaw that takes full advantage of the space. The different levels of the platform combine with the walkway to create sufficient space for two bedrooms, closets, and a bathroom area. The range of colors is deliberately restricted by the choice of materials: wood for the horizontal surfaces and white for the walls. The kitchen is set underneath the platform, and the bedroom module is separated from the living area by glass, allowing natural light to enter. In this loft, the use of space has been calculated down to the last inch; the result is an expansive home flooded with light, where one space flows into the next.

Architect: Choon Choi Design

Location: New York, USA

Completion date: 2004

Photographer: © Paul Warchol Photography

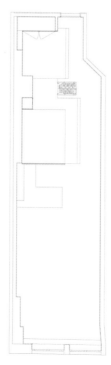

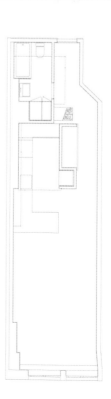

Plans

The different levels of the platform make it possible to set two bedrooms in the upper area, even though the total height available would not allow room for an additional story. The loft has been left open, to take advantage of sunlight, but subtle divisions succeed in differentiating the spaces. A glass wall serves not only as a safety feature but also separates one bedroom from the kitchen, as well as leaving on show the structure of the mezzanine.

The metal staircase is situated between the two bedrooms on the platform; it also serves to differentiate areas on the lower level, such as the entrance to the bathroom and one of the closets. The metal finish adds a contemporary, industrial touch that recalls the staircases found on ships. Its gradient and placement provide space for the side corridor.

Axonometry

Brantschen Apartment

624 sq.ft.

This apartment is located in the heart of Lausanne. The rigid interior structure, dating from the 1950s, was modified to create a much more flexible space. First, the partitions were removed, except those in the small bathroom, so that, at the express desire of the owners, the space was more open. One of the most striking features is the bookcase that separates the living room from the bedroom: this sliding unit can create settings of greater or lesser privacy, expanding both spaces while also providing great storage capacity. Other mobile panels make it possible to close off the kitchen from the other parts of the house. The wooden parquet, partially retained, brings warmth to the apartment and sets up a gentle contrast with the modern furniture.

Architect: Concept Consult Architectes

Location: Lausanne, Switzerland

Completion date: 2004

Photographer: © Pierre Boss

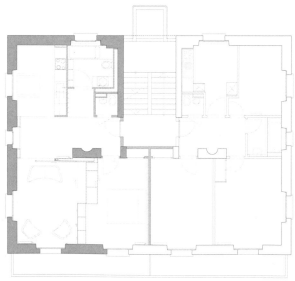

Plan

The translucent material used for the sliding panel allows the light that enters through the windows of one room to penetrate into the others. The mobile shelves and closet serve a double function: they provide storage space and separate two areas.

Lina House

635 sq.ft.

This unit, originally conceived as a small extension to a family house, is in fact completely autonomous and contains all the services required for a self-contained home, currently occupied by a woman and her daughter. The limited floor space, coupled with financial restrictions, determined what type of construction was possible, and it was finally decided to design a module that could easily be removed or enlarged in the future. A glass wall floods the interior space with light, as well as opening it to the exterior—a wooded area on the grounds of the house. White is the predominant color inside the house, endowing it with a continuity that is broken only by dashes of color on the furnishings and in the bathroom. The floor is made of pale wood throughout the house, adding warmth to the setting.

Architect: Caramel Architekten

Location: Linz, Austria

Completion date: 2004

Photographer: © Caramel Architekten

The large glass wall opens the home on to the exterior and allows sunshine to enter, making the most of the daylight hours. The trees and lush vegetation of the garden surrounding the house can be observed from the comfortable living room, or shut out by means of large drapes that serve to make the interior more intimate.

The half-height furniture fulfils various functions in these small spaces, providing storage facilities and making the rooms seem bigger. This commode with simple, straight lines helps create fluidity. The wooden floor adds warmth, while the predominance of pale colors conveys a sense of calm and harmony.

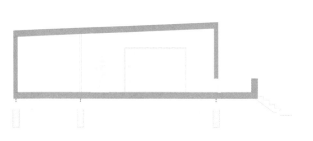

Section

Plan

Ivory Fresh Shell

635 sq. ft.

The Black Treefrog building in the middle of the Austrian town of Bad Waltersdorf is made up of several striking apartments. One of these, known as Ivory Fresh Shell, is a combination of different spaces pointing toward a central "neutral" area measuring 194 sq. ft. The bathroom, kitchen, dining area, and living room—all measuring 150 square feet—can be opened or closed according to the needs of the moment, to such an extent that the apartment can come to seem empty. This home exemplifies versatility, thanks to the ingenious furniture design and the well-handled layout. According to the architects, the useful space is multiplied when the space of all the areas is added together. The upper floor, containing the bedroom and another bathroom, is another small, original space that marries practicality with innovation.

Architect: Splitterwerk

Location: Bad Waltersdorf, Austria

Completion date: 2004

Photographer: © Paul Ott

The main characteristic of this apartment is the way that its various areas are hidden behind doors or mobile panels. The occupants can find themselves both inside an empty cube and seated on a comfortable couch. The rooms can appear or disappear very easily, demonstrating that versatility is the greatest virtue of this project.

Occupying a former Chrysler factory, this loft was designed by Marie Veronique de Hoop Scheffer, an interior designer from Belgium. Captivated by the city of Buenos Aires and inspired by the astounding glacial landscapes of Patagonia, she discovered the Palacio Alcorta, which contains some of the most beautiful lofts in the city behind its neoclassical façade.

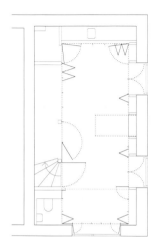

Lower level

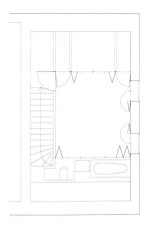

Upper level

Light Frame

645 sq.ft.

This space was originally a studio in an art school fitted with a skylight that allowed sunshine to pour into the large room below. A refurbishment reduced the size of the skylight and divided the space into five small rooms, but this project sought to recapture the luminosity and restore the unity of the original space. A new opening, almost sculptural in its forms, was put in the roof; its L shape crosses the roof and emerges as a glass, cube-shape bar on the upper terrace. Inside, the bathroom is situated under the skylight and is closed off by polyester panels that allow the artificial light used within to be seen in the lounge both by day and by night. A unit containing the kitchen, office, and other service areas is the only component in this setting bathed in light.

Architect: Gus Wüstemann
Location: Zurich, Switzerland
Completion date: 2004
Photographer: © Gus Wüstemann

The bathroom is the only enclosed
space, as it requires privacy; however,
the materials used for its construction
allow the sunshine entering through
the skylight to gently and subtly filter
into the interior. The studio's warm,
delicate atmosphere was achieved by
means of translucent materials and the
interplay of artificial and natural light.

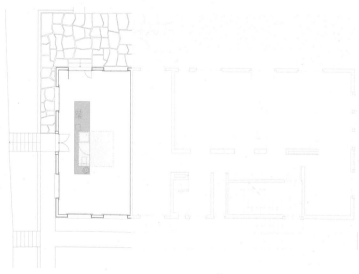

Plan

Slit Villa

721 sq.ft.

In Tokyo, architects must adapt more than in most cities to spatial restrictions and find ways to draw up houses of limited dimensions without sacrificing aesthetic values. This three-level house is a good example of a combination of functionality and visual attractiveness. The contrast between traditional materials like wood and more modern ones like steel reflects an important trend in present-day Japanese architecture. The exterior shutters, made of bamboo (another prominent material), determine the look of the spectacular façade; these folding roller blinds are translucent and set up a link with the interior. Similarly, the interior glass panels make it possible for the different areas of the house to establish visual relationships between each other.

Architect: Chikara Matsuba/Tele-Design

Location: Tokyo, Japan

Completion date: 2002

Photographer: © Ryota Atarashi

The bamboo shutters bestow intimacy on the interior of the house without losing contact with the exterior, as they are semitransparent. When they are folded back, light pours inside and makes the interior seem bigger, while exposing it to view from the street.

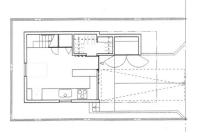

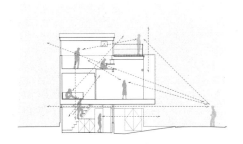

Section

Plans

Elevation

Glass is one of the outstanding elements in this house. It is overshadowed by the bamboo roller blinds on the façade, but it comes into its own inside, where it succeeds in establishing continuity between the various spaces, even when they are set on different levels. The bedroom is characterized by its brightness, a result of the placement of the window.

Option

742 sq.ft.

Option is a model for a prefabricated house, built out of wood, at a minimal price but with high-quality finishing. It is a module that can function as an independent home, studio, or annex to a main home. The structure is assembled in a factory and the definitive installation can be completed in a single day; as it is a modular construction, the two initial levels can be modified or extended. The interior space has been exploited to the maximum to take full advantage of every inch, and the area devoted to transit has been reduced to a minimum. Similarly, four windows add a sense of expansiveness and brightness. The communal areas are situated on the ground floor and the private spaces, such as bedrooms, on the top level.

Architect: Bauart Architekten

Location: mobile

Completion date: 2002

Photographer: © Andreas Greber

Hasle-Ruegsau/Weberhaus

The large window brings light into the rooms and provides visual continuity. In this way, the home opens to the exterior while also forming part of it, as well as contributing to the sense of spaciousness.

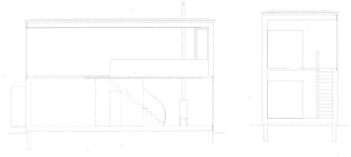

Sections

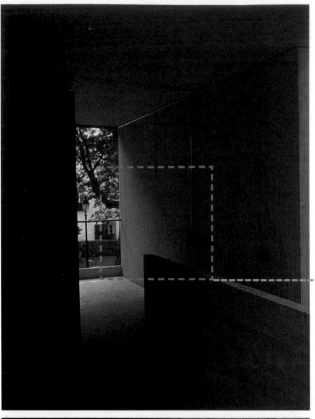

The transit areas have been minimized to take advantage of the space; the staircase leading to the upper level, for example, occupies very little space. The decoration on the floor with the bedrooms is minimal, but the light from the exterior combines with the wood to create a warm, tranquil atmosphere.

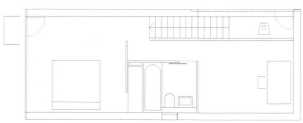

Upper level

Lower level

Ground Floor

753 sq.ft.

Although the refurbishment of this apartment on the ground floor of a two-story building led to a modernization of the space, every attempt was made to preserve the original house's rustic feel. The vaulted ceiling was retained and tiles were put on the floor. A translucent sliding door separates the bedroom from the lounge, expanding the space when it is pushed back. The lounge also contains a small kitchen and dining room. Blue is present on the ceilings, in the kitchen, and on the cushions on the terrace, contrasting with the warmth of the wood, floor, and furniture. Ornamental elements bestow character on a home, serving to define its style, and in this project they have been chosen with special care to give cohesion to a simple but appealing decoration.

Architect: GCA Architects

Location: Barcelona, Spain

Completion date: 2000

Photographer: © José Luis Hausmann

In the kitchen, the electrical appliances are set on panels, thus achieving a total integration in the space; the kitchen's position, between the lounge and bedroom, turns it into a transit area, so it must always be free of obstructions. The table serves as both a work top and an eating area; the chest of drawers can be pushed aside to seat more guests, if necessary.

Ground Floor

Decorative elements must be chosen - - - - - - -
with particular attention, especially in
small spaces, to avoid looking cluttered.
In this case, wooden bookcases fixed
directly to the wall prevent an
accumulation of books and other
objects in the living area. The lamps
point to the ceiling to create diffuse
lighting that brings warmth to the
setting.

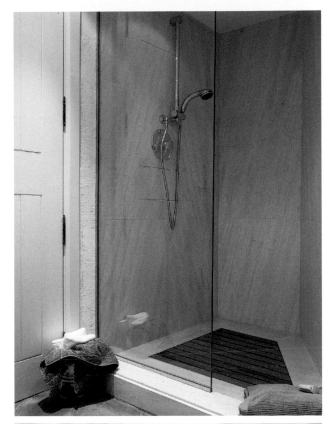

The door that opens onto the patio is broad and therefore allows sunlight to penetrate into the house, as well as providing a connection with the exterior; in summer, the patio can be considered an extra part of the house itself, a small lounge, with cushions on the floor to create an informal, festive, and youthful atmosphere.

Rectangular Floor Plan

753 sq.ft.

The refurbishment of this New York loft sought to respect the industrial spirit of the original space while equipping it with modern domestic facilities. Its special atmosphere has been preserved thanks to the way the different areas have been laid out; the building's structure demanded functional solutions, so walls and enclosed spaces were dispensed with—except in the bedroom and bathroom—to gain fluidity, and the natural light that enters through the large windows heightens the feeling of spaciousness. Similarly, the brick walls and wooden beams have been restored, and antique furniture has been introduced, to contrast with the modern kitchen and bestow character on the loft.

Architect: Alexander Jiménez/
Abaton Architecture
Location: New York, USA
Completion date: 2000
Photographer: © Jordi Miralles

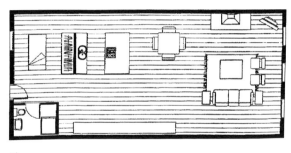

Plan

The brick wall evokes the building's original industrial use and makes the loft a welcoming space, as the wall serves as a decorative element in its own right. The strong presence of the brickwork is balanced and softened by the presence of medium-height bookcases.

Organic Spaces

764 sq.ft.

This small apartment, which belongs to one of the architects from the team, had to provide continuity between the spaces and a peaceful atmosphere with just a few touches of color and finishing of the highest quality. The lower floor contains the living room, dining room, and service area, while the upper floor is given over to spaces that demand more tranquility and seclusion: the bedroom and the studio. The partitions ensure intimacy without renouncing a unified approach to space, and the minimalism of the setting conveys serenity and restfulness. The furniture, all made of wood, is sparse, with very pure lines that accentuate the apartment's simplicity and endow it with a warm, organic feel.

Architect: Claesson Koivisto Rune Arkitektkontor

Location: Stockholm, Sweden

Completion date: 2000

Photographer: © Patrick Engquist

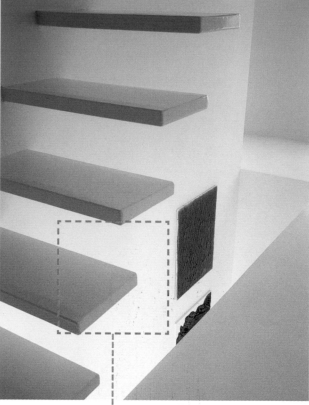

In order to occupy as little space as possible, the staircase going up to the top floor is fixed to the partition separating the dining room from the living room. Its lightness and linear simplicity are striking, as they make it look as though the staircase is unsupported; it has been painted the same white color as the walls to integrate it into the structure of the building.

Kenner Studio

775 sq.ft.

The Kenner studio is a small house with a garden that belongs to a director of documentaries and his family. Its structure is defined by the garden and a main residence of historical importance situated close by. Sheets of birch wood were used for both the floor on the lower story and the walls on the upper story, as well for covering the façade; as a result, the living room is surrounded with wood and a visual connection is established between the interior and the exterior. The design of the rooms avoids any superfluous elements and is confined to simple lines to avoid disrupting this dialogue. The interior seeks to satisfy the needs to divide the space and control light and sound, as well as fulfilling the desire for visual communication with the exterior.

Architect: Fung-Blatt Architects

Location: Los Angeles, USA

Completion date: 2004

Photographer: © Deborah Bird

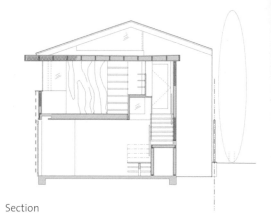

Section

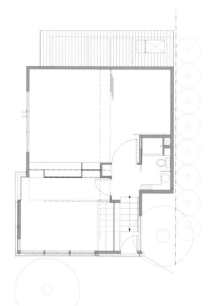

Lower level

Upper level

The sliding glass doors open the living room onto the exterior, turning it into a kind of porch; the couch offers views of the exterior, creating the sensation that the trees and vegetation form part of the house. The birch-wood sheets covering the façade are also visible from the interior, adding warmth to the entire house and creating a peaceful, relaxed atmosphere.

Apartment in Casa Magarola

775 sq.ft.

The refurbishment of an old seminary in the historic center of Barcelona resulted in some small homes (including this apartment) with a structure proper to a loft. High ceilings, spaciousness, abundant sunlight, and pleasant surroundings are just some of its selling features. One of the main aims of the decoration was to create a warm, inviting setting, and this was achieved through the strategic distribution of artificial light and the thoughtful selection of colors for the couches, drapes, and carpets. The bathroom is situated in an enclosed area, with the bedroom set on a platform above it, and in this way both spaces enjoy privacy. Two mobile wooden panels hide or reveal both a big closet and the kitchen, thereby changing almost completely the appearance of the large sitting room.

Architect: Jordi Solé Ràfols
(of the remodeling of the building)
Designer: Bárbara Salas
Location: Barcelona, Spain
Completion date: 2000
Photographer: © Montse Garriga

Sliding doors are a very useful resource in small homes; they are easy to integrate into the architecture, making it possible to modify settings by revealing or hiding spaces. In this case, the large wooden panels not only add warmth but also integrate the kitchen into the dining-room area.

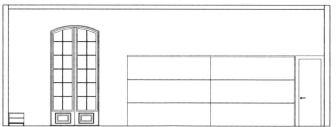

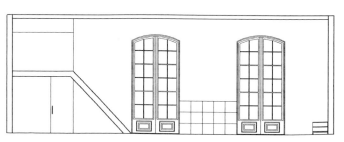

Sections

The wooden beams and parquet floor create a welcoming atmosphere. The use of polished steel establishes a contrast, however: the center table and couches are just some of the elements that have metal structures or finishing, offsetting the warmth around them to provide a more modern, urban look.

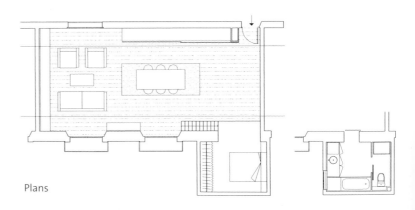

Plans

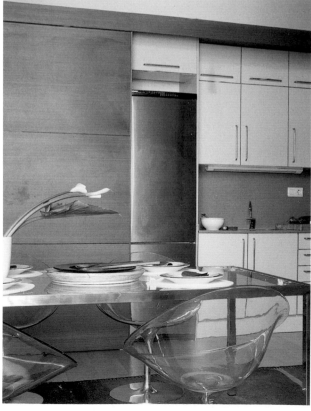

The double height at one end was exploited to make room for the bathroom and bedroom. The metal structure separating the two levels is exposed to view and also functions as a decorative element. The small staircase—also made of metal—that goes up to the upper floor has a streamlined appearance that perfectly matches the look of this loft.

House in Tokyo

796 sq.ft.

Achieving privacy was one of the objectives of this project, as this small house is surrounded by houses only a short distance away. The solution was to insert a skylight—so that sunshine could enter the house—while fitting side windows at a sufficient height to block views from outside. Sunlight floods into the interior, producing a sense of spaciousness without sacrificing intimacy. The first floor contains the daytime area, dining room, and kitchen, while the bedroom and bathroom are down below. The wooden floor brings warmth to a space with a minimum of furniture and barely any decoration; the architecture is also of a minimalist nature, and it has found ingenious ways to create an ample and comfortable residence.

Architects: Takaharu & Yui Tezuka/ Tezuka Architects, Masahiro Ikeda/Mias

Collaborators: Masahide Kakudate/Masahide Kakudate Lighting Architect & Associates

Location: Tokyo, Japan

Completion date: 2002

Photographer: © Katsuhida Kida Photography

The white closets produce a similar effect to that of the wall, integrating all the elements of the living area. This low furniture, situated on either side of the dining area, provides storage space and adopts a subtle presence while maintaining the minimalist aesthetic that dominates the entire residence.

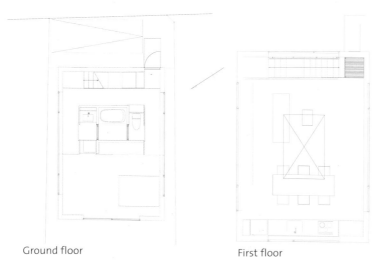

Ground floor

First floor

Apartment in Brighton

796 sq.ft.

This early-twentieth-century apartment was refurbished without any detriment to the authenticity of the original structure, although it was adapted to modern requirements. The living room has lost none of its grandeur, and some of the moldings have been retained; various modifications were also made, however—the high ceilings were exploited to add a studio, with the bedrooms set underneath. The bathroom and kitchen were also renovated, using glass instead of bricks in the upper part of the walls to allow light to enter from other parts of the house. The decoration is minimal, but a modern atmosphere has been created with the elements derived from the refurbishment, and from the fiber-optic lamps that stud the ceilings throughout the house.

Architect: Knott Architects

Location: Brighton, UK

Completion date: 2001

Photographer: © Knott Architects

Glass has always been a major ally in small spaces, as it can serve to separate different settings while also allowing light to pass through them. One of the kitchen walls was replaced with glass in order to increase visibility and continuity with respect to the other spaces. Similarly, the decision to give the walls a curved finish instead of an arris heightens the modern look of the apartment.

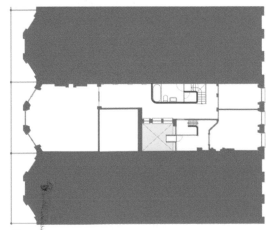

Plan

One hundred and forty-four small fiber-optic lamps are scattered over the ceilings of the entire house, creating an almost magical effect that greatly alters the perception of light and space; by night they glimmer like stars and are multiplied in the reflections of the mirrors in the bathroom and kitchen.

Taylor Loft

796 sq.ft.

This small three-floor loft has access to a roof with views of Hollywood and Los Angeles. The original idea was to refurbish only the kitchen, but it was eventually decided to add the upper floors. One of the first steps was to remove all the elements that marked off the space in order to divide it afterward with suitable materials. The most noteworthy aspect of this project is undoubtedly the furniture, adapted to the needs of the owners, which helps to define the different spaces according to their function. Bamboo has been used for the transit areas, cement for humid areas, and cork tiles for the living room.

Architect: Joshua R. Coggeshall/Cog Work Shop

Location: Hollywood, USA

Completion date: 2004

Photographer: © Deborah Bird, Cog Work Shop

The design of the furniture is one of the most striking aspects of this project. The living room shares the same space as the kitchen, but all the areas are distinguished visually by the use of a particular material. The furniture in the sitting room is designed with clean, simple lines that hide a wealth of small storage spaces.

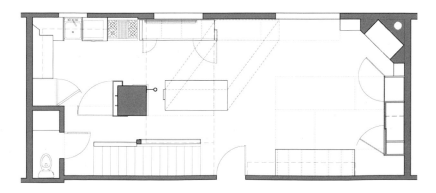

Plan

Dwelling in Barcelona

807 sq.ft.

The refurbishment of this apartment mainly involved eliminating as many walls and doors as possible—the kitchen and bathroom are the only areas that can be closed off—and thereby creating a sense of greater spaciousness. The original arch and pillars were retained, to visually separate the lounge from the bedroom and also to establish a contrast with the modernity of the rest of the elements in the house. The metallic gray of the couches and dining-room table add a touch of serenity to the living area, while the bright colors in the bedroom combine with the layout to establish a very warm atmosphere. This harmonious setting is rounded off by the entrance of natural light.

Architect: Nacho Marta

Interior Designer: Jorge Rangel

Location: Barcelona, Spain

Completion date: 2000

Photographer: © José Luis Hausmann

A large tatami in the bedroom provides extra space for personal objects, as well as serving as an intimate lounge area. The counterpane, cushions, and candles create a cozy atmosphere at night, while by day sunshine filters through the drapes onto the white walls to suggest warmth and tranquility.

In the bedroom, a sliding door separates the bathroom from the closet, thus respecting the need for privacy while also ensuring that clothes, shoes, and other personal objects are out of sight. Small spaces must not have too much furniture, but as a result they tend to present storage problems; fitted closets or sliding doors are often the best solution.

Engawa House

807 sq.ft.

This small rectangular building has a large glass wall, 20 feet long, with nine sliding doors that can be pulled back to open the house to the exterior and turn it into a large porch. All the various parts of the house are visible from the outside, as if they formed a large store display. The house is situated in front of another residence belonging to the same family; the two buildings are directly linked by a patio, which also serves as a communal area. The wall opposite the expanse of glass is lined with fitted closets that maintain order, a very important factor in small spaces. The luminosity and the layout of the furniture produce an effect of continuity and expansiveness. All in all, the personality of this house is defined by balance, simplicity, and warmth.

Architects: Takaharu & Yui Tezuka/ Tezuka Architects, Masahiro Ikeda/Mias

Collaborators: Masahide Kakudate/Masahide Kakudate Lighting Architect & Associates

Location: Tokyo, Japan

Completion date: 2003

Photographer: © Katsuhida Kida Photography

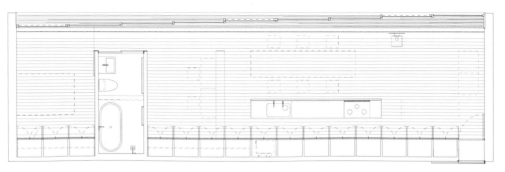

Plan

The interior is one open space—apart from the bathroom, which is the only room endowed with more privacy. Shelves in the dining room mark off the office, which also serves as a child's bedroom. Simplicity and versatility are also key factors in the achievement of functional, well-arranged spaces.

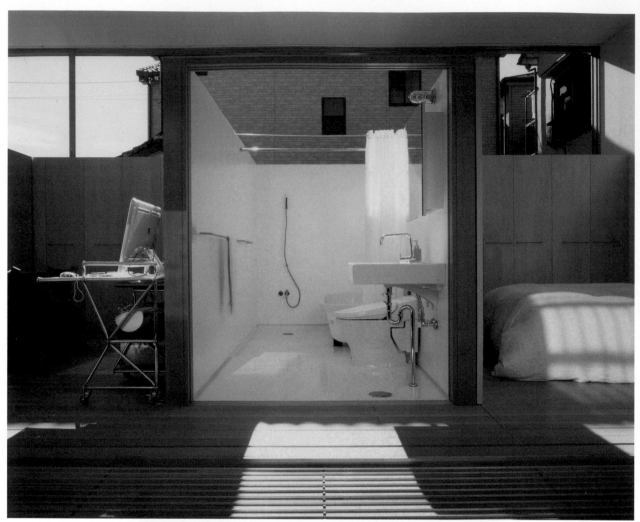

Mukarov House

807 sq.ft.

The Mukarov House is built on land covered with trees, which leaves little space for construction. This made it necessary to design a house spread over four levels, to gain space on the vertical plane. The relationship between the garden and the interior is one of the outstanding features of the design. Glass walls and large openings have been inserted to allow natural light to penetrate into the interior, although the north and south façades have no windows, to protect the interior of the house from the rigors of the climate, and to provide greater intimacy. The interior space is totally continuous and the furniture elements serve several different functions.

Architect: Ivan Kroupa

Collaborator: Radka Kurcikova

Location: Prague, Czech Republic

Completion date: 2000

Photographer: © Matteo Piazza

The use of a single space for various purposes can sometimes be a response to a necessity rather than a whim. The versatility of the furniture makes the different areas more spacious; the mobile walls and units can be rearranged to allow the living areas on each floor to adapt to their specific requirements.

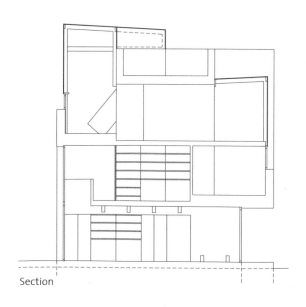

Section

The four levels are linked without any interruption, to create fluidity. The vertical composition makes it possible to see above the garden to the landscape beyond. The interplay of natural and artificial light sets off the spatial geometry and brightens up the setting.

Annalisa Loft

861 sq.ft.

The refurbishment of this loft involved converting two different apartments into a single home. The preexisting structure lacked any aesthetic or architectural value, so the idea was to strip it away, leaving the brick wall and arched vaults exposed, allowing in more light and endowing the space with greater expansiveness and personality. Another consequence of the restructuring was that the night-time area was set on the upper level, thereby achieving greater intimacy. The daytime area became a single space taking in the living room, the modern kitchen, and the bathroom. The decoration plays a significant role, as it adds character while avoiding the industrial austerity and minimalism typical of many lofts. Similarly, the lighting creates a warm atmosphere, while some of the accessories, such as the bathroom mirror, reveal the distinctive taste of the owner.

Architect: Studio Del Portico

Location: Milan, Italy

Completion date: 2003

Photographer: © Andrea Martiradonna

Lighting is one of the elements that best defines the style of this loft; whether by making the bathroom mirror glow or by using candles in the living room, it sets up a play of shadows that imbues the loft with great personality. The original combination of lamps gives a unique touch to each of the living areas, helping to create different atmospheres.

Seewald Residence

893 sq.ft.

This small house on a mountain, surrounded by nature and blessed with superb views, is a family vacation home. The project sought to create a simple, streamlined architecture, organized around four interconnected rooms. The square floor plan and wooden structure recall a typical Alpine cabin. Four large windows make it possible to contemplate the landscape; in summer, they can be kept open to establish even more direct links with the exterior. The atmosphere inside is cozy, despite the austerity, as the choice of furniture and use of wood have resulted in a small, serene and welcoming setting, an ideal place for recharging the batteries.

Architect: Marte Marte Architekten
Location: Zwischenwasser, Austria
Completion date: 2000
Photographer: © Ignacio Martínez

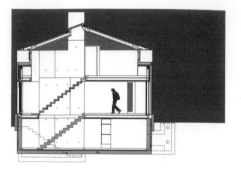

Section

Basement

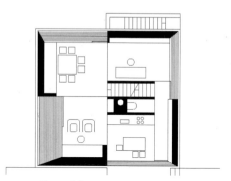

Ground floor

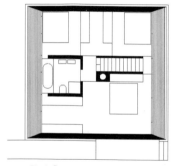

First floor

The interior combines both cold and warm materials. The wood exudes comforting coziness while the metal adds a more modern touch to the bedroom. The side window and skylight in the roof make the room seem brighter and more spacious, counteracting the effect of the low roof and wood cladding.

Darmós House

904 sq.ft.

Darmós is a small town in a rural Mediterranean setting surrounded by pine trees and vineyards. The project involved the refurbishment of an old house in the town; the result was a small independent residence on the top floor. One of the outstanding features of the renovation is the fact that one of the wings of the roof has not been rebuilt and the space has been used as a terrace, with views of the fields and the town. This has resulted in more space outdoors and an abundance of light indoors, entering through the terrace door and window. Although the distribution of the spaces and furniture is modern in style, the interior is imbued with a rustic atmosphere, on account of the original stone walls and the simple decoration.

Architect: Joan Pons Forment

Location: Darmós, Spain

Completion date: 2003

Photographer: © Eugeni Pons

The small kitchen, with its views of the terrace and the exterior, is set practically in the center of the home, backing on to the eating area. The layout of the kitchen has been calculated down to the last detail to make the most of the available space and all the modern conveniences without sacrificing floor space or functionality.

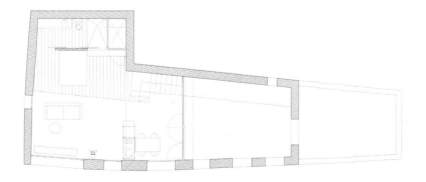

Plan

Windows substitute for walls in some parts of the home, as the considerable height allows them to be very large, meaning that the interior can receive abundant sunshine. Even the small bathroom area, which backs onto a party wall, enjoys natural light and seems spacious.

Attic in Barcelona

936 sq.ft.

The abundance of natural light is undoubtedly the main feature of this attic in Barcelona. The privileged location of this house and the glass walls in some rooms allow sunshine to pour into every nook and cranny. The white walls and simple lines of the furniture further enhance the sense of spaciousness. White in fact predominates—particularly in the kitchen—but a few splashes of color have been added via the wallpaper to avoid coldness or monotony; similarly, dark wood has been used for the parquet floor and the bathroom furniture, to contrast with the paleness of the walls and couches. Wood and bold colors are also present in the bedroom, resulting in an inviting, intimate space.

Architect: Àlex Serra

Location: Barcelona, Spain

Completion date: 2004

Photographer: © José Luis Hausmann

The walls of the living room are made entirely of glass. Roller blinds and thin drapes make it possible to preserve intimacy without losing light, while also creating an atmosphere replete with serenity. As this attic is high, it enjoys stunning views of the city.

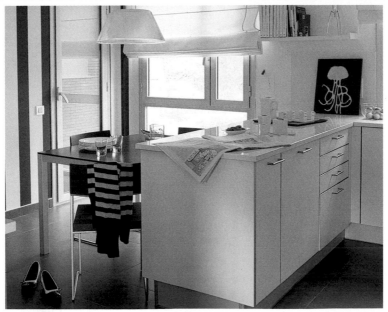

Smith Apartment

947 sq.ft.

A three-room apartment was turned into a two-room home complemented by a studio (which doubles as a guest bedroom). All this was achieved without sacrificing elegance and spaciousness. A large stone bench provides a workspace in the kitchen, while also separating it from the dining room. The wall of the sitting room is occupied by a lacquered gray closet with a large storage capacity, used to keep electrical equipment. A system has been developed to allow paintings to be hung in front of the least used parts of this closet. The details of the decoration are modern and the materials unobtrusive, allowing the art collection and the spectacular views of the city to capture the attention.

Architect: Smart Design Studio

Location: Sydney, Australia

Completion date: 2002

Photographer: © Sharrin Rees

Plan

The steel-framed glass panels, the work of the artist Janet Lawrence, offer a practical means of separating or uniting the studio and the sitting room. It combines with the other artworks to create a comfortable, peaceful atmosphere, thereby attaining a perfect marriage of simplicity and stylishness.

House in Bilbao

958 sq.ft.

The main aim of this refurbishment was to find room for a workspace for the owner, who is a professional musician, while ensuring that the installation of this soundproofed room did not prevent the rest of the space from functioning as a home. The music studio was set in a cube, and a sloping wall was erected: these are undoubtedly the most striking interventions, as they completely alter the perception of the home, endowing it with personality and, as they are freestanding, also bringing fluidity and continuity to the space. The rest of the rooms revolve around it. The modern layout of the rooms contrasts with the preexisting wooden beams, and further variety is achieved by the presence of furniture in different styles.

Architect: Carmen Abad Ibáñez de Matauco

Collaborator: Cristina Pedrós (architect)

Location: Bilbao, Spain

Completion date: 2004

Photographer: © Alberto Martínez

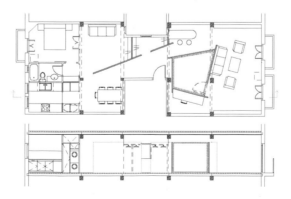

Plan

The cube containing the music studio is the most eye-catching part of the home: it manages to be central and isolated at one and the same time. The soundproofing not only prevents the music played inside from being heard in the rest of the home, it also allows the owner to work in peace, undisturbed by external noises.

Locher Apartment

968 sq.ft.

The building in which this apartment is set dates from the 1970s and is located in an industrial neighborhood. The anonymous exterior contrasts with the owner's desire for individuality indoors. The aim of the refurbishment was to turn a standard four-bedroom apartment into a spacious loft. Fortunately, it was blessed with the ideal conditions: abundant light and a structure that made it possible to remove walls. The apartment had to include all the required services while giving priority to a relaxation area and an organic visual approach. The most eye-catching features of this home include a large, upholstered wall that hides the kitchen and bathroom, and an elegant bathtub that serves as the central dividing element and a symbol of relaxation.

Architect: Spoerri Tommen Architekten

Location: Zurich, Switzerland

Completion date: 2004

Photographer: © Michael Freisager Fotografie

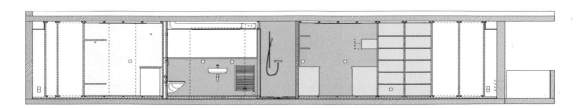

Section

The kitchen, bathroom, and other areas lie behind the upholstered wall. Each space is a different pale color. The bathroom, for example, is painted blue and the kitchen, pink. The soft color scheme and minimal decoration imbue the apartment with the desired atmosphere of relaxation and tranquility.

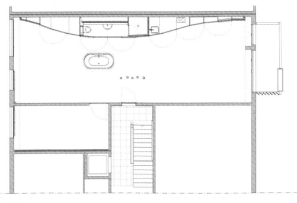

Plan

Apartment in Milan

968 sq.ft.

This apartment is set on the top floor of a building originally designed as a company headquarters and subsequently converted into a residential block. The owner, an Englishwoman resident in Italy, needed a space in which to live and work, while also allowing her to put up visitors. The refurbishment eliminated all the partitions to leave a large open space bounded only by the outer walls; the idea was to create a more private nighttime space between two daytime areas: the sitting-dining room and the studio. The masonry walls marking off the rooms do not reach the ceiling and have openings that facilitate the circulation of air and the entrance of light. The upper floor—a small garret with a guest bedroom—is reached through the studio.

Architect: Luca Rolla

Location: Milan, Italy

Completion date: 2002

Photographer: © Andrea Martiradonna

The masonry walls divide the various areas in the daytime areas. One of them forms a corridor that leads to the living room and another separates the kitchen from the dining room. These openings are also present in other rooms—the wall between the bathroom and studio—and provide uniformity and continuity throughout the apartment.

A wood and metal staircase links the studio to the guest bedroom. It rises between the bookcase and the table, but its simple lines and lightness make it an element that is both functional and decorative. The simple decoration in the studio stands out against the minimal furnishings and the teak parquet, which adds a touch of warmth.

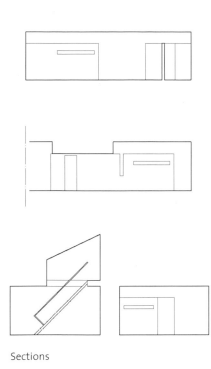

Sections

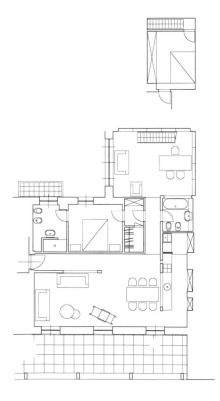

Plans

The Hammer

968 sq.ft.

The aim of this project was to create a loft in an old attic in Zurich with magnificent views of the lake, the city, and the wood. The first step was to turn the roof into another usable space, so this was treated as if it were floor space. The pale walls and ceilings set up a dynamic contrast with the dark beams and furniture. The main characteristic of this project is the structure that has been inserted into the loft—a hammer linking all the main areas: the office, balcony, bedroom, bathroom, and closets. Instead of creating specific settings, these areas are connected to each other according to their relationship with the hammer. There are no walls in the normal sense of the term; spaces are defined only by being behind, inside, or next to the hammer.

Architect: Gus Wüstemann

Location: Zurich, Switzerland

Completion date: 2004

Photographer: © Bruno Helbling/Zapaimages

The contrast between the dark beams and the white ceilings combines with the striking indirect lighting to bestow personality on the loft. The interior spaces are not marked off by conventional walls, and the loft's structure is left exposed, creating a free composition in space, with special emphasis on the ceilings and beams.

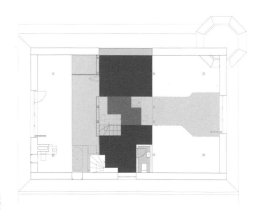

Ground floor

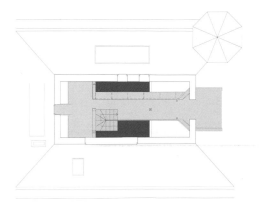

First floor

White is another outstanding feature, as it has been applied to both the walls and some parts of the floor. This increases the sensation of clarity and spaciousness; any potential coldness is offset by the addition of carpets and natural fabrics. The decoration is completed with original furniture, which enhances the personality of this home.

Loft in Gràcia

968 sq.ft.

Architect: Albert Danés Tejedor
(of the remodeling of the building)

Collaborator: Maria Alejandre Galiano
(interior architect)

Location: Barcelona, Spain

Completion date: 2000

Photographer: © José Luis Hausmann

The recent transformation of Barcelona's urban fabric has meant that some former industrial neighborhoods have now become residential areas. The building in which this home is set was converted from a factory making electrical appliances to a block with loft-style apartments. The refurbishment was distinguished by its simplicity, and a similar criterion governed the interior design, which resulted in one single space plus a bedroom. The outstanding features are the kitchen, open to the lounge, and the evident desire to respect the building's industrial appearance. The interior was improved with a change in the color scheme and lighting, along with the installation of high-quality parquet. The vaulted brick ceilings and the metal structure evoke the building's past, while the new additions reflect the adjustment to the changing requirements of the neighborhood.

The kitchen opens on to the lounge, thereby contributing to the sense of expansiveness. The use of bricks in the bar emphasizes the intention to evoke the loft's industrial past, and, as is customary in this type of home, there is a contrast between the coldness of the structural elements and the warmth of the decoration.

Directory

René Dekker
C14 The Old Imperial Laundry
71 Warriner Gardens
SW11 4XW London, UK
T. +44 020 7622 4777
F. +44 020 7622 3663
M. +44 078 7603 2631

White Architects, White Design
Box 2502
403 17 Gothenburg, Sweden
T. +46 316 08 600
www.white-design.se
www.optibo.se

Rolf Åsberg
Örlogsvägen 73
42671 Västra Frölunda, Sweden
T +46 31 291080/+46 52351650
M +46 708 291180

João Maria Ventura
Rua da Madalena 139, 2º
1100319, Lisbon, Portugal
T. +351 21 395 4566
F. +351 21 395 4566
jmtrinidade@mail.teleweb.pt

Gary Chang/EDGE
663 King's Road
North Point, Hong Kong
RM 1706-08
T. +852 2802 6212
F. +852 2802 6213
edge@netvigator.com

Hiroaki Ohtani
Chuo-ku, Osaka, Japan
T. +81 6 6203 2361
F. +81 6 6203 4277
ootani@nikken.co.jp

Studio Associato Bettinelli
Via Carrozai 6b
24122 Bergamo, Italy
T. +39 35 235796
F. +39 35 225941
betinellistudio@bitbit.it

Luigi Colani, Hanse Haus
Ludwig-Weber-Straße 18
97789 Oberleichtersbach, Germany
T. +49 (0) 97 41 8 08-0
F. +49 (0) 97 41 0 08-119
www.hanse-haus.de

Werner Aisslinger/Studio Aisslinger
Oranienplatz 4
10999 Berlin, Germany
T. +49 30 31505400
www.aisslinger.de

Smart Design Studio
632 Bourke St.
Surry Hills NSW
Australia 2010
T. +612 8332 4333
F. +612 8332 4344
www.smartdesignstudio.com

Studio Uribe - London Miami
411 Fulham Palace Road
SW6 6SX London, UK
T. +44 20 7731 1420
1225 Lenox Avenue
Miami Beach, FL, 33139, USA
T+1 305 695 1415
pablo@studiouribe.com

Jeremy King
27 Maldon Road
W3 6SU Londres, UK
diggie.king@btinternet.com

BEHF Architekten
Kaiserstraße 41
1070 Vienna, Austria
T. +43 1 524 17 50 0
F. +43 1 524 17 50 20
www.behf.at

Studio Rodighiero Associati
Piazzale Resistenza 12, Castiglione d/S,
Mantova, Italy
T. +39 0376 638883
F. +39 0376 671187

Wingårdh Arkitektkontor
Kungsgatan 10ª
411 19 Gothenburg, Sweden
T. +46 (0) 31 743 7000
F. +46 (0) 31 711 9838
Sjövikskajen 16
11 743 Stockholm, Sweden
T. +46 (0) 8 447 4080
F. +46 (0) 8 744 4005
www.wingardhs.se

Peter Hulting /Meter Arkitektur
Kolonigatan 4
S- 413 21 Gothenburg, Sweden
T. +46 31 20 43 30
F. +46 708 910 310
www.meterarkitektur.se

Massimo d'Alessandro & Associati
Via delle Mantellate 18/b
00165 Rome, Italy
T. +39 06 68 33 529
F. +39 06 68 33 532
studio@dalessandroeassociati.it

Rafael Berkowitz/RB Architect
445 west 19 street 6f
New York, NY 10011, USA
T-F. +1 212 691 5922
www.rbarchitect.com

Guilhem Roustan
22 rue de la Folie Méricourt
75011 Paris, France
T. +33 1 43 55 80 04
F. +33 1 40 21 69 14
guilhem.roustan@free.fr

Roger Hirsch
91 Crosby Street
New York, NY 10012, USA
T. +1 212 219 2609
F. +1 212 219 2767

i29 Office for Spatial Design
Industrieweg 29
1115 AD Duivendrecht
Netherlands
T. +31 20 695 61 20
F. +31 20 416 57 05
www.i29.nl

Choon Choi Design
150 W 28th Street, Suite 1801
New York, NY 10001, USA
T. + 1 212 255 5250
www.a-scape.com

Concept Consult Architectes
Côtes de Montbenon 16
CH-1003 Lausanne, Switzerland
T. +41 21 351 30 50/52
F. +41 21 351 30 51
info@concept-consult.ch

Caramel Architekten
Schottenfeldgasse 72/II/3
A-1070 Vienna, Austria
T. + 43 (0) 1 596 34 90
F. + 43 (0) 1 596 34 90 20
www.caramel.at

Splitterwerk
Mandelstraße 33
A-8010 Graz, Austria
Kamperslaan 17
NL 2624 Delft, Holland
T. + 43 316 81 0598
F. + 43 316 81 059840
www.splitterwerk.at

Gus Wüstemann
Köchlistraße 15
8004 Zurich, Switzerland
T. +41 1 295 6013
F. +41 1 295 6019
M. +41 79 634 73 40
Rambla 73 2° 3ª
08002 Barcelona, Spain
www.guswustemann.com

Chikara Matsuba/Tele-Design
2-12-5 Openstudio Nope
Mita Minato-ku
108-0073 Tokyo, Japan
T. +81 3 3769 0833
F. +81 3 3769 9893
www.tele-design.net

Bauart Architekten
Laupenstraße 20
3008 Bern, Switzerland
T. +41 (0) 31 385 15 15
F. +41 (0) 31 385 15 10
www.bauart.ch

GCA Arquitectes
València 289 bajos
08009 Barcelona, Spain
T. +34 934 761 800

Alexander Jiménez/Abaton Architecture
10-41 47th Avenue, No.3
Long Island City, NY 11101, USA
T. +1 718 482 1458
F. +1 718 482 1459
M. +1 917 647 5884
abatonarchitecture@earthlink.net

Claesson Koivisto Rune Arkitektkontor
Sankt Paulsgatan 25
118 48 Stockholm, Sweden
T. +46 8 644 58 63
F. +46 8 644 58 83
www.claesson-koivisto-rune.se

Fung-Blatt Architects
104 N. Avenue 56
Suite 3 A
Los Angeles, CA 90042, USA
T. +1 323 255 8368
F. +1 323 255 3646
www.fungandblatt.com

Bárbara Salas
Goya 14 1° 2ª
08012 Barcelona, Spain
barbarasalasbcn@hotmail.com

Takaharu & Yui Tezuka/Tezuka Architects, Masahiro Ikeda/Mias
1-19-9-3F Todoroko Setagaya
158-0082, Tokyo, Japan
T. +81 03 3703 7056
F. +81 03 3703 7038
www.tezuka-arch.com

Knott Architects
98B Tollington Park
N4 3RB London, UK
T. +34 207 263 8844
F. +34 207 263 4700
www.knottarchitects.co.uk

Joshua R. Coggeshall/Cog Work Shop
6000 Monte Vista Street
Highland Park, CA 90042, USA
T. + 1 323 719 22 65
jrcogg@pacbell.net

Nacho Marta
T. +34 93 731 4285
Jorge Rangel
Lafont 22
Barcelona, Spain
M. +34 616 515 279
jorgerangel@terra.es

Ivan Kroupa Architects
Gonkarenkova 10
Prague 4
Czech Republic
M. +42 0 775 106 816
F. +42 0 244 460 103
www.ivankroupa.cz

Studio Del Portico
Viale Col di Lana n° 7/a
20136 Milan, Italy
T. +39 02 89406644
F. +39 178 602 8592
delportico@tiscali.it

Marte Marte Architekten
Totengasse 18,
6833 Weiler, Austria
T. +43 5523 52587
F. +43 5523 52587 9
www.marte-marte.com

Joan Pons Forment
Cervantes 7 2° 1ª
08002 Barcelona, Spain
ponsforment@coac.net
M. +34 670 856 261

Àlex Serra
Pau Alcover 92 2°
08017 Barcelona, Spain
T. 134 93 2119537
M. +34 670 232 121
asdesign@retemail.es

Estudio de Arquitectura Carmen Abad
Calle Padua 97 sobreático.
08006 Barcelona, Spain
T./F.+34 93 212 31 51
estudio@carmenabad.com

Spoerri Tommen Architekten
Gertrudstrasse 24
8003 Zürich, Switzerland
T. +41 01 451 01 02
F. +41 01 451 01 34
spoerri.thommen@everyware.ch

Luca Rolla
Corso Venezia 8
20121 Milan, Italy
lucarolla@katamail.com

Albert Danés Tejedor
Verdi 187
08024 Barcelona, Spain
T. +34 932 181 272
F. +34 934 160 096
albert-danes@coac.es
María Alejandre Galiano
Travessera de Gràcia 147 1°
08014 Barcelona, Spain
T. + 34 932 375 903
marialejandre@telefonica.net